I0172865

VIA Folios 124

Packs Small Plays Big

Packs Small Plays Big

Phyllis Capello

Bordighera Press

Library of Congress Control Number: 2017959137

Cover Art:
Luciano Capello, House Paint on Burlap

© 2018 by Phyllis Capello

All rights reserved. Parts of this book may be reprinted only by written permission from the author, and may not be reproduced for publication in book, magazine, or electronic media of any kind, except for purposes of literary review by critics.

Printed in the United States.

Published by
BORDIGHERA PRESS
John D. Calandra Italian American Institute
25 West 43rd Street, 17th Floor
New York, NY 10036

VIA FOLIOS 124
ISBN 978-1-59954-108-2

to M, S, & J

Contents

Overture

*"One does not choose
one's subject matter,
one submits to it."*
Flaubert

For some there's a poetry that sings the names of trees,
provides lyric scrutiny of wildflower bloom,
speaks calmly of country lanes,
the caw of migrating birds over ancestral fields;
this is not for me; my landscape rattled with rage,
subway trains, apartment house windows
lit at night against the windy gloom.
There was, shining above water tanks,
a star or two.

Good children wanting to be happy
try to drown the kettle drum's roll of doom.
Our fancies, our jabbering *pizzicato* filled up
already crowded rooms; in this place
we were taught self-exile, were witness
to a mother's descent from woman to ruin.

Once, at dusk, glancing up from my homework page,
I saw our fifth floor neighbor's leap from her sill,
arms spread wide, her form a dark and silent bloom.
Your work is bleak my mother-in-law says:
write about nature, the eyes of children,
sunsets—*cartoons.*

This, as I begin to learn what it is
makes a woman fracture, come
undone in the midst of din; this,
as the walls around me ring—*what is
that racket my children are making?*

Tell the girl, humming
and bent to her books, hopeful that will
can sustain her: I understand now—melodies
live longer than girls;
a woman is falling still.

Fate

The silver moon talking
That was my curse

The summer night
skipping over dark sand,

she spoke above the drone of waves:
Embrace him, she commanded;

but the seabirds started squawking,
I couldn't hear the rest.

Selfish crone, how could you
doom my innocence?

exile a heart from radiance,
to wretched winter's cold abyss?

The Goddess, Six Days a Week

for Lisa

Toward the end of the long subway ride
from Queens to the nail salon,
the subway pulls itself up a curving track
rushes out of a long black tunnel
into stark Brooklyn light; that's the moment
a homesick Nepali immigrant, half-asleep between
the lurch and screech, could mistake
bright morning sun on a high train platform
for a white mountain peak.

Later on, if her mind drifts for an instant
from chattering customers
and chemical stink, she could,
hefting my warm wide foot
from the soapy basin, be lifting
her own baby from a bath
in the kitchen sink.

Still bent to her work when the sun sets,
the evening customers come; she paints
their toenails Himalayan crimsons,
her tiny gold bracelets, tinkling
like prayer-bell reminders, make her think
of her last call home, the breezy way she's learned
to croon: *It won't be long now, Darling!*
while her little boy weeps into the phone.

She doesn't know I'm the daughter
of the son left behind in Sicilian hills,
how, for his passage, my grandmother
repaid the loan shark with piecework,
thousands of miniature buttonholes, and lace
like snow, sewn onto baby clothes.

At the nail salon her boss says:
*Hurry up, girls, tips in the can
and use your American names!*
Then the door slams.

On the radio the newscaster says:
soldiers and protesters crowd
the streets of Katmandu!
The goddess has no green card,
she shrugs and smiles,
lifts pretty hands to heaven:
I make and send, she says,
I make and send.

A hundred years ago workers
blasted, burrowed into the deep,
but at that one high station because tall-masted ships
sailed the old canals beneath, they made the track
exit the earth, so now, the train chugs to the top
of the silver rail and the goddess, son faraway
in Nepal, new daughter asleep in her womb,
holds tight to her purse, blinks in the blue
above the Brooklyn streets, on the arc
near the splendid harbor,
where the glimmering city reappears.

A Stranger to the Story

Poseidon's hounded him; he's just washed ashore
on his remnants of raft in a god-rage made storm;
and soon King Alcinous' unsinkable fleet
goes to a terrible end trying to sail him home.
He'll tell us, after he cries, that despite Calypso's
many charms, the nightly lovemaking,
he wept gallons trapped on her isle.

How is it a naked shipwrecked man receives,
not just the rags and scraps he begs,
but a princess' interest, her sage advice
and a purple tunic woven by a queen?
Was he as alone as he seemed?
Gray-eyed Athena turned village-girl
to point him through Phaeacia's maze of streets.
Didn't he swing open the palace gates boldly,
for a sea-tossed captain without ship or mates?

Honored guests are bathed, rubbed with oil,
roasts and breads prepared, Odysseus
made his libations from the king's side,
so why hide, sobbing—lustrous fabric
drawn across his face—as the blind rhapsod
sang of Troy, when it was he who'd asked?

No one sees his own actions; we're blind
as we live them, at home, or on the battlefield;
in story they're reborn; Homer makes him weep
not during his hardships, the loss of friends,
but as a man at the banquet with an appetite
for words; every warrior going out young,
knife in hand, has a name; wise kings know
when to ask, and to invite a poet to the feast
who returns to us in song the immensity
of what we haven't seen in what we've done;
oh, for a tunic at a time like that!

A Night's Sleep

for M.

Remember: you've slept on,
and tumbled off
the precipice, risen
from sleep and sleeplessness,
and lived to work again

There are times you turn out
the bedside lamp and rush (ragdoll limp
and smiling) off the day's brink;
times you trip off: eyes closed, arms apart,
falling asleep in the air.
But then you wake in the dark,
to the rattle of pipes,
the window in its frame, the child
crying out in fear; alarm jangles
your dream-warmed bones;
the good sleep in your blood
pivots like an army and marches
back toward wakefulness.

If this happens it's best
to resist the swift velocity of thought
          (which will, like a giddy partner,
dance you further from rest, unravel
the heavy fabric exhaustion has knit,
each fancy step, another row
of careful stitches ripped.)

Deafen yourself: to the voracity
of children, the city and its citizens,
sister's telephoned sighs, the boss's
rubbery mouth and sputtering lies;
let sound fade like the fallen mountaineer's
last, untethered, spiraling cry;
and draw sleep's black ink
down into your bones.

Factory Girls, Bangkok

In the morning country girls (on their way
to city jobs) ride the rickety bus
over the steep green hills.
All the way to the factory they chatter
like a treeful of birds.
Soon, their quick brown fingers,
their bright, sharp eyes,
will feed cheap fabric to furious needles;
dart by dart, seam by seam, piles of dresses
and sleeves will rise up beside
their clattering sewing machines; they'll work
as if bewitched, till dark.

Yesterday, the dawn, rising over
the far mountains, was mirrored
in the still lake; but today there is deep fog;
the bus, gears grinding, winds its way
down slick roads; the air is wet
and dense against the windshield.
Girls, at a nearer stop, huddle in the mist,
wave dim flashlights, board,
like a family of ghosts.

Each one carries a small packet of lunch,
a tube of lipstick, a plastic comb
to smooth down her sleek black hair.
A homely girl, voice rising happily,
reads aloud from a movie magazine.
Every now and then she stands and holds
the glossy photos high above her head.

This afternoon when the explosion
rises—an enormous roar
over the drone of machines,
and the windows splinter—millions
of needles sailing off into
the air like glass bullets,
when the raging fire obscures
every exit save one, hundreds of girls
will go running and screaming

through the terrible heat,
the stinging black smoke.
Tomorrow they'll find the youngest ones,
dead by the dozens: tiny wrists,
small clever fingertips crushed,
trampled by their rushing sisters,
till they have no breath to rise
and move—like the half-grown
flowers they are—toward the light.

Memory Speaks

for R

Enfolded, pupa in white sheets, dying Vladimir
told Dmitri a certain butterfly, "on the wing,"
would have to flit unwitnessed that year.
A chrysalis can hang through a brutal spring

defying gales, April's fierce rains, until
precisely the moment nature says: flutter out!
Go find a proboscisful
of nectar! Old writers know how-

ever captured or catalogued, a span is brief;
perhaps a lusty zigzag before the end of it;
then the net descends, you're pinned, a painted leaf
put in a box your flight forgotten bit by bit.

What can an artist say about the radiant whole?
There once was a day, a walk in the grasslands,
a packet of sandwiches, Vera's good-bye smile,
her kiss in the evening when she took our hands;

moonshine over fields of folded wings as false-eyed
moths came twirling past! That's enough to tell:
not that ardor ends; that ardor's still inside
every silken, soon-to-be discarded shell.

Poetry Homework

Determine if the angle of youth is > than
or < than the angle of loneliness.
Explain why brain chemicals often = self-delusion.
Discuss whether hubris remains
forever undivided by experience.
Here are the facts:
It was summer + he was handsome.

If a pretty girl (#1), purposefully enlarges
a chance encounter with (oh, let's call him 2),
is it because she's inventing emotions to pass the time?
How then can these factors be resolved?
        a) 1 + 2 + the baby = happily ever after 'til The End?
        b) 1 + (baby) - husband = poverty (+ new loneliness)?
Either way, it was a beautiful night!

So, if 1 + 1 = 3, then 2 leaves, will there still be 3 wholes?
It's all right to use your fingers.
After a (9 month long) parentheses
Baby 3 was born!
Her eyes shone like the morning star!

Which phrase best completes the thought:
It's possible to be happy even after:
        1) the moon is removed from the sky?
        2) Baby Morning Star grows up without a father?
You may make a grid, shade in, or leave blank:
        a) broken halves of the hearts
        b) the empty portion of the bed

What else could have happened when a girl
from an avenue called "X," seduces the wrong unknown?
State, in your own words, how young couples
all over the world still have the same longing.

In your poem be clear from the first kiss,
in the dreamy way she holds his hand and
adds her name to his; use details!
the moon shining down on the bench, hum of traffic
whizzing by, how they could ever believe
they were the center of the universe,
sitting near an avenue absurdly called "Y?"

How Women Get to Hell

With some it is circumstantial:
familiar terrain reconfigures, one
misstep and lives disassemble:
illness manifests, husbands vanish,
children spin wildly off into darkness.
The certainty of loss is bitter on their tongues
as they descend.

Others march there,
fancied up, lusty enough
to kiss the devil; the gate
swings open, destiny
turns the key.

Some marry the devil,
spend lifetimes exchanging
immense effort for small affection,
terrified silence for perilous calm.
They enter meekly, bereft of thought,
empty of notions.

But the young ones,
because they are blind,
or blithe or beautiful,
seem to find the path no matter
which way they turn;
that slippery golden path,
which takes them, smiling
and unsuspecting, to the brink
where they stand, pretty toes
pointing down, ready
for the push.

Songs in the Life Cycle

In the high school bathroom mirror the girls
sing the *Hope-He-Notices-Me-First*, song, the
His-Lips-on-Mine; laughing, they draw dark lines
around bright eyes, press on bright lipstick.
I teach them poetry, which won't pay the rent
like waitressing can, or marriageable bodies might.

Mother and I sing over my comatose aunt
helping her die in the dowdy hospital
not far from the institution; beyond words now
we croon Italian melodies drowning the ventilator's hiss,
our bodies tilting toward hers:

> *Oh memory! sweet summer night, long ago!*
> *her murdered sons alive! scrambling over*
> *Grandpa's low stone wall clutching for fireflies*
> *to fill my empty jar.*

The childless are chanting on the uptown bus,
eyes closed, as the fertile board with their radiant children;
they are chanting as Saint Anne passes on her parapet,
carried, block by block, as in ancient times, by females
of her tribe; with silent lamentation the childless reach up—
to touch the hem of her robe, every woman's
invocation pinned there in gold.

My daughter hums in her tiny flat, rent unpaid,
as sirens scrape the already-jagged landscape and traffic
shifts and halts making the music of gears and brakes.
See her standing in her window, in Hopper-light,
young breasts beneath thin fabric, heart and mind on fire,
watching the city for signs.

Old woman alone in her dusty apartment,
dependent on neighbors' attentions,
the company of disinterested cats,
she too, watches from her window.
See her every Friday recounting her tales
with the coins in the paperboy's palm.
But at night in her bath! each splash

against a wrinkled thigh reminds her
how once touch traveled skin to heart,
and oh, the beautiful rhythms of love!

In the labor rooms women are singing—
gasping and keening in a rain of sweat.
Riding the dark hurricane of pain, of life
desired, conceived, contained, bearing
the fruit of the moon; the war of wiles
is waged for this: crescendo,
finale, reiteration.

The nurses are singing in the station,
sharing news of death and life and lipstick shades;
they tap-tap their syringes, cha-cha to
the scratchy radio--what words? they laugh—
what words--to that old tune?
Always the youngest ones holding fast
the smallest babes too sick for home.

I am singing, in the phone, as my daughter
sighs in her window, two month's rent due.
Picture her—thin blouse over white skin,
rose-red lips, shining eyes taking in
evening's last breath, the ever-changing din.

"Can you sing a song now, Mother?
my belly rumbles, the sky darkens;
I watch from my tenement window as the girl
with a ponytail like mine skips rope in the alley;
will I have a child? pretty women
with painted mouths are passing—have they come
to steal my new love?
Across the way an old woman with no one
is touching herself!
The city we love is killing us,
Mother! Quick, a song—some harmony,
to practice in the mirror—to sing in ecstasy
and terror, as siren and lover, in sing-song
and rhapsody, in wonder—Oh, Mother,
that star up there! is that it? is it wonder?"

The King of Sleep: A Lullaby

*"My sleeping is my dreaming,
My dreaming is my thinking,
My thinking is my wisdom."**

Dormeus, in darkness I shake off my clothes,
I loosen the pins from my hair,
I shiver—but I do not fear you, Dormeus.
Oh, Beast—if you come when the nightingales
fall silent, such stars will there be in my window
and I will lie silvered by the moon!
Come and place here, in the curve
of my throat, your black rose.
For one night of bliss: my promise
is this: a million tales of love
and breasts that are satin to your lips.

Beast, I am still sleepless—*where
have you gone?* I call you, come!
It is I—who sing your name
in the Library of Dreams—who,
for the drug of sleep have learned
to pay in song!

> Let me wake in a roomful of jewels, in a hall hung with silk,
> in a garden of flowers, in a chamber fragrant with honey,
> let me wake a queen—your black arms the throne.

> *A dormire, dormire, dormire,
> dormo, dormate, dormiamo,
> dormirò, dormirò, dormirò.*

**The Great Earth Mother Erda
in Wagner's "Gotterdammerung"*

The Dancing Girls of Derry

The new cruise ship, tethered in the gray harbor
like a giant swan, is the first one here in years.
In high hopes the town council sends girls
to the seldom-used dock; a chorus line
of red-cheeked lasses bob under the awning stripes
to charm the tourists come to gape and shop.

Our passengers, just returned from scenic drives,
line portside, ignoring the Irish rain,
the lunch announcement chimes.
Crew in aprons, coveralls and kilts
stop their tasks to watch.

Today the city hall staff served us tea;
the mayor raved about scones,
not the blast, that last week
sent three to their tombs.
Near the road sign that says: "*You're Entering
Free Derry*," laborers wave and jeer;
the tour guide edits her text;
our bus rolls past the ruins.

In a tumult of jig and horns
our ship pulls away from the wharf;
there are tears; cameras click and whir;
then the dancing girls halt their rat-a-tat-tat;
the workers turn back to their chores.

Tonight the ship's band plays from its list;
the passengers gesture with forks.
We leave it all behind: the British sentries
armed in barbed wire forts, the mayor's lure
of girls and scones; how next week's walk,
on the old town wall by a Protestant boy
may make grown men brave bullets with stones,
and the glorious music that powered the dance
which we breathed in like hope,
like gulps of fine sea air.

Demeter's Undoing

Persephone was abducted, taken
from the light, but some daughters
go willingly; renaming the darkness
love, they step down.

He bought her with trinkets, an ounce or two
of affection; her heart fluttered; she did not
recognize the serpent's twist in his smile.
The night he told her disobedient girls
were buried in the mountains she dreamed their bones
glowed in the dark earth like weak lanterns, that
their peasant fathers cried out to the Madonna
and crossed themselves as they floated by.
So, when the devil bent to unlace her shoes,
she did not object, and went two days barefoot.

The morning he returned, parcel of new clothes
in one hand, vanished shoes in the other,
she put aside her dreams and lay with him.
Shivering, she rose to dress,
this time he bent to lace her shoes.
They drove through the village; the mothers
hurried their daughters away; everyone knew:
he was the wicked prince in the golden coach,
she, his expendable princess

Quick as gold spun from straw, heroin hidden
in shoes has made him rich; but when this
señorita arrives (the airport dogs run,
sniffing and yelping at her heels) she yields
to the customs' search.

In the old story domination
is a metaphor for passion.
The long narrow windows of the county jail
shimmer at night; cell by cell,
each woman recalls her passage: the politics
of arousal, the consequence of persuasion
the sad, seductive, foreplay of submission.

Full Moon Talisman

It is October, past midnight; I lead the way
to the amphitheater through the back streets
(less twisting and narrow than the inner labyrinth
that winds through town) even though
your Athenian family always vacationed here;
and I wonder now: Did your mother
have her instrument then on those
breezy Mykonian nights? as I always have mine?

You hadn't told me yet, saved it for our last day
when we stood at the bow and the old ferry churned toward Delos.
She died in my arms, you said, offhandedly, as if to the waves.
On the island you were buoyant again,
greeted the museum guard by name; we hiked
among the ruins, picnicked where Ledo had her twins:
Artemis, whose ghostly beams bring easy death, came first;
mighty Apollo was second-born there,
in that most sacred of caves.

Mykonos was full of tourists when we returned;
we were silent in the port café; then you went on ahead
to thread a way through the noisy crowd.
Then you stopped, spun around in that swirl of passersby,
I read such wildness in your eyes: *She brought*
her little mandolin to school, you said, *sang*
to her students! knowing full well that's what I do.
A few minutes later we have to say good-bye.

It is cool when we walk to the theater,
a strong breeze rifles cascades of bougainvillea
spilling over the old stone wall, turning
from the path we step first into a nave
of utter darkness, then find ourselves walking,
as if from one dream to another, into silver moonlight
directly on the stage—you become
Orestes—enraged! Win, with Aeschylus' words,
heaven's permission for your matricide.
I didn't tremble when you shook your fist at the sky,
but when it was my turn to sing my little song

and you looked up at me with those blue eyes.
Here is the tragedy my friend: how we—with all our talents,
are cursed and clever children still, uncertain when,
instead of acting, we have to tell about our own lives.

Goddesses

For is not every woman a queen—
who goes out into the darkness
and brings back light?

Gioia Timpanelli, on *Vasilisa the Beautiful*

"Little mother," I address the terra cotta figurine
in the archaeological museum in Athens, "how big
your eyes are!" Her left arm holds a child,
its head and her breast are one form,
a sphere unbroken except for a thumbprint's
slight indentation, "even at your age,"
for she is surely just a girl, "you *know*!"
This is the year I've lost my menses.

As the tourist bus winds it way back to our ship
a woman tells me her teenage son has just ceased
his cancer treatments; we invoke the polysyllabic names
of poisons, late twentieth century incantations
and her eyes, icily composed before our words,
become liquid-blue, bright as the Aegean we'll sail on today.
"All of it," I say, patting her woman-sized back,
"takes such courage."

That evening, at the captain's dinner, the geologist
leans over my plate to reprimand: "*Gold*,
he tells my new bracelet, "*is the earth's blood!*"
Across our table sits the recently-widowed doctor,
her face lost in an ocean of thought.
Yesterday, as I handed the sales clerk my money,
I noticed this childless pediatrician, scanning
the jewelry store's treasure, absently stroking
her wedding ring, wishing her love alive again.

That moonless night we meet on deck,
the amateur astronomer's lamp spans the heavens;
under the stars we wonder where in Time we are:
I'll send no more prayers to Artemis, goddess of childbirth;
the blue-eyed mother holds hands with her precious son;
the doctor, draped in a shawl, lifts her dreaming face;

charting our ways, will we look back on this night?
when we floated in the sea—black and silent and huge,
joined, like points of celestial light,
by the same stories, our faces upwards.

Last Night's Lunar Eclipse

I slept through the whole thing;
my writer friend set her alarm,
stood in the backyard
in coat and slippers,
"Beautiful," she said, "despite clouds."

Videos show earth's round shadow
vanishing the moon.
"Not since the solstice of 1638 . . ."
newscasters expound, jabbering on
about "umbra," the "blotting out of light."

In front of the 24/7 store,
the old sock man waves bouquets at me:
white socks blooming in one grimy hand,
black ones drooping from the other.

Three-hundred-and-seventy-two-years from today
shake the poet awake, tell her:
please buy the socks a peddler sells:

Terrestrial needs first.
A man is singing, to you,
in the beer sign's pink light:

"Lady, lady! Five pair!
Five *pair*! Lady: *Only three dollars!*"

Packs Small Plays Big

Magicians say it about certain props:
the doves, silks, feathered headdresses,
that spring into exuberant life
from a tiny packet.

Bach unfurls, too; melodies
scatter skyward, or fold up,
The Milky Way kept in, or whirling out,
of a pocket.

On stage it's gold coins plucked from air,
milk-white doves fluttering up;
feathery flick and our magician goes
from tux and tails,
to Indian chief.

On the country driveway
Will tells me about a shooting star
and I find myself on a road
in dark woods.

Misdirection, skill,
a hinge of words,
the small swing that can play big;
we don't see it happen,
then there it is.

No One Escapes Aphrodite

Tell, Muse, how we lay
on a dirty beach as if on a silken bed!
Remind me that the moon lit my lover's face
and pushed me toward him; we traded
intimacies, as the young do, while behind us
the sea swelled and a city
was hushed to nonexistence.

The world became his hands
making the shape of my wrists, my breasts,
white foam my hips; the dance unfurled;
for all it cost, the tears, I blame
the sea; memory breaks
at its crest to wash over me.

Questions for the Rose

Shall I betray you rose?
if I say you were lit as if a flame
this noon while we gasped and gaped
and snapped away to capture
your red soul in our brief stay?
Sure, your red is so red our idea of red
is not red enough but if you resist recounting
who'll know how
your coil of perfect petals
burned my eyes in the just past
morning light of June?

Guitar in the Garden

Woody smell of old strings on fingertips;
birds listen, whistle, listen.
You're here, too. I play so quietly, you say,
clicking on a long string of colored lights
to make the ferns silver up.
Your blossoms in their little pots, like the tall oak,
all still now; neighbors laugh through wooden fence.
A plane flies east past the crescent moon;
won't be long till we say: What, full again?

Diner Haiku

TV cameras catch
Grieving woman being led
Past the homemade shrine

Public Pool

flipper-flappers
friend-splashers
little jumpers
big ploppers

baby-huggers
baby-tossers
orange-haired
whistle-mouth

the citizens are wet today

The Background Manifests the Figure

Pawnshops, donut shops, cops,
dumpsters, indoor mall of posh chain stores:
What's on your want list? asks a big sign.

A neighborhood of twenty eighteen-story buildings,
each one named: Rome across from laundromat;
Paris looms over fried chicken shack;
London looks down at liquor store, pizzeria.

At the first turn-your-gold-into-cash store
a bald pamphleteer hands me an ad;
a tall man by the other store bobs
up and down in a sandwich sign;
the bent woman in the discount doctor's entryway
squints; plastic bags blow by us
in fifty mile-an-hour winds.

There's a public library in Australia,
furthest building from the subway stop
and expressway ramp;
sign on the door says: "*Saturdays & Sundays Close!*"

Seven students in my afterschool poetry workshop
in The Meeting Room, near The Teen Room,
(just shelves of fashion magazines,
six old computers and the six
fastest boys from the junior high).

We start with oral tradition,
why Rock-a-Bye-Baby is a good poem.
"Maybe," a boy says, "maybe,
at the last moment,
the baby's rescued by birds?"

When the librarian's assistant sits in,
she shows us how, with a little yellow pencil,
a broken-hearted woman, can write a poem
that turns the straw of her life
into gold; no wings; just words.

Walking Into the Dream

Part I.
Here, In the City of Women

Out in the streets, the streets,
the bloodstained streets, night presses in
all dark and breath--a beast:
          Bone-rattle, infant-cry, night-siren moan—
my address, in the neighborhood of bones.

A white swan-moon sailed past our home tonight,
all shimmer and ice, but blind
to my heart's fight; a wand'ring eye adrift,
(unloving blank) it pulled (rattle and clank)
we rose and sank.

My son's still a boy
but rapidly grows, my bold daughter
through these bloody streets, roams;
and I am me and them and us and I;
and I am us and them and me and I;
and we have all been kissed and loved and wronged;
all of us have tripped and mourned and longed.

What savoring is left, of lost-love's spoils?
when what is left of flesh on bone,
recoils? (*Oh, the streets, the streets,
the bloodstained streets—no tears can bless,
no work, this maze, completes!*) With what
pointed words do we scratch out our graves?
          I want to, I won't; I love you, I don't.

I record this brief and bleak surviving
as death (his bony knock) is just arriving.
Rattle and infant-cry, night-siren moan: Here,
In the City of Women, my home.

****

Part II.
The Maid

I dreamed this dream on my mother's feet,
firstborn, first friend, first foe,
then friend, complete;
she carried me adrift in reverie;
adrift in reverie, she carried me.
In dreamtide do the dreamer's feet touch earth?
And, Mother, before I walked on your feet,
did you dream me, first?

So I step, into my song, my self, my grave;
my step is Time and with each stride I fade,
and reappear: a girl, a crone, a maid.

> We tossed our dreams, rough stones,
> into the dark sea's raveling and unraveling;
> city-children, encamped on dirty beach,
> hypnotized by firelight; we measured
> the leap of flames, the depth of promises.

> Swimming in the cold night air,
> my silkie surfaced; by the fire's gleam
> his grin chose me.

> (Flowing in the moon's currents, scavenging
> the physical, was I a mermaid then?
> dizzy on the heart's-zigzag, diving
> to his blanket-cave; playing at the ritual?

> All wildness gathered into me:
> the tolling ache, the fire's race,
> the windy sea; all, found their place
> along my willing shelf.)

> Over girlish shoulders spilled my inky hair,
> my urge both grace and curse, laughing
> I rode his rhythmic hips, seducing myself, first.

****

Part III.
The Beast in His Labyrinth

The crow's cough,
the laughing caw, calls
me down the dreaming-street.

Into the wilderness of flowerpots and garden hedge
heel, sole, toe, I go, marking
the crisscross of pretty streets and hideous streets
that stretch, catlike, in undulant mystery,
like a skin of shifting stone, this zigzag-city,
coasts upon a gulping monster's back;
just to get a taste of us—*It licks*
around the windowbox, all along the
the ridge of here-and-now.
Beware—*It's* putrid breath
can poison even marrow: "Do not rise up!
'Ten-Thousand-Mouths-That-Cause-A-Mother's-Sorrow!'"

But, searching tips of pointed tongues are ravenous
among the darling ones, lapping up
the rose to leave the thorns.

****

Part IV.
The Babe

We all revolve, the grandma
and the babe, the steps not
taken, and all the choices made.

Blame hummed in mother's glance
eddied 'round the cupboards, slid
under jambs, and found us where we hid:
frightened innocents, quaking lambs.

Untethered pearl of their lover's act,
sailor-girl from her velvety sac,
once I was a sperm dance jig in father's pants,
filled with his passions and his ignorance, but
married to their loneliness (little bride
of circumstance) wasn't I the perfect frame for sorrow.

****

Part V.
The Walk

The crow's cough,
the laughing caw, calls
me down the windy street.

All actions—sanctioned! A blessing
on all faces, my soul: unfurled,
my step: a glide, not counting paces;
a time between, an idle breath, the mind
swept clean of intellect: oasis.
Wait, what dread tongue is lapping here,
rising up from memory's intersect—what poison
threatens, what midnight fear—Monster,
have I not sung enough?

And now what, Mother,
do I wait or walk? Father,
should I lace up
my tongue, or talk?

****

Part VI.
The Lovers

Traffic's blurred hum,
crow asleep on leafy bough,
crickets' creak-a-creak, dark
presses down; row houses repeat.

Behind blued panes: lovers, in their beds, reach;
in the rising and falling of flesh, in
the mingling of skin, in the curve
of breasts they speak, lips on lips;
her hair inside his fists.

He has licked her long eyelash,
how she has laughed! Each hair
is dear to her: nape and stubble and groin;
she whispers: yes! gathers up in her caress:
the press of dark, his thumping heart,
row-house-repeat, cricket's secret
creak-a-creak, crow on the branch, asleep.

In this drowsy ease they sleep; the city's
held-breath, holds them;
side by side they dream, of children
and monsters.

****

Part VII.
The Crone

Behind a silvered-pane a ghost-face floats:
old sentry, at her bedroom-window post,
Guardian of bric-a-brac on windowsills
(souvenir ashtrays, commemorative vases, and there,
by the plastic Vatican trinkets—a shepherdess figurine
flirts, gathers up her lacy, frozen skirts, and turns
a painted-rosy cheek, from the shepherd-boy's
forever undelivered kisses.)

A mirror? in our eye, the same
tear, the same stare? watching over
this street, aware, *aware.*
Philodendron spirals green to her arthritic knees,
cars whiz blindly by, what does this witness see:

> *Designed and redesigned: dark worlds,*
> *the intense porch-games of little girls;*
> *theories lisped and artfully involved;*
> *quick conceived, and just as quick, dissolved.*
>
> *Her old eyes trace and then retrace,*
> *the harmless madman's metered pace*
> *(like a meditative skater's blade*
> *on ice) his feet, in holey shoes,*
> *describe a pattern: a personal,*
> *relentless, lemniscate, invisible upon*
> *the darkening street; an earthly dance,*
> *performed on dreaming feet.*

******

Part VIII.
The Words

She carried me
adrift in reverie; adrift
in reverie, she carried me.

In dreamtide do the dreamer's feet touch earth?
And Mother, before I walked on your feet
did you dream me first?
Watch me step into my song and self
and grave; my step is Time and
with each stride I fade and reappear:
a girl, a crone, a maid.

Monster rising up,
to lick the roses off the thorns:
where are the darling ones?
gone? to kiss and love and
mourn and long?

The crow's cough, the laughing caw,
calls me down the dreaming-street,
walk onwards, walk on words,
walk without words.

Pasiphae

Once on Crete's abundant shore
Minos asked Poseidon for a sign:
Out of the blue swam a luminous bull,
milky white as stars!
Blinded by such magnificence,
the story goes, Minos put
a lesser bull to death instead
and went from king to cuckold.

But what if, all the while,
the bull were meant for Pasiphae
and not the fire? after all, Asterios
was a king himself and her power
harkened back to *Magna Mater*.
So perhaps his radiance was contrived?
not as honor's test but to wake
a sleeping queen's desire?

Never mind that she was a woman
and he a bull; everyone here is a coupling
of human and beast; and rutting madness
always finds a way—just look around you!
The ancients said a bull's horns
were twin new moons; he mounted her
as a cow on Crete's white shore but Pasiphae
was The All-Illuminating, The Glimmering One,
Daughter of the Sun and Moon; Daedalus'
contraption of wood and hide was her disguise.
She waited in the dark within as a queen
and bride, not the first woman or the last
who has made for herself a different skin
and climbed inside.

Jumper Cables

for L.

Winter? Wasn't it yesterday
I trampled magnolia blossoms delighting
in the sidewalk crunch, composing
some sing-song poetry crap in my head?
It's the end of a long workday,
I'm tired, cold; my old car; parked
by the cemetery fence; won't turn over.

I call my brother to come and rev
his engine into mine; then, chirpy with appreciation
I prattle on; through the crack of the raised hood,
I see some new uncertainty has blurred
his features into silence; so I will myself
to think instead of how the long purple clouds
blow across the low red sun.

Behind us the el arrives, screeching,
which makes the station shake,
then the train huffs and hisses away
dragging its clacking chain along
the steel horizon; the wind picks up;
I shiver; isn't there still a lot of sky
above these graves?

And where's the nod to turn the key?
give another crank, and damn
the starter? Where's our spark,
that turns this lifeless heap
to sputter? to turn the sputter into hum
with zip enough to let us both
drive away tonight, if not, tomorrow?
put a little distance between this gusty,
incremental dark and that damned
twittering bird, crow or sparrow?
that keeps jabbering *whatcanitbe?*
whatcanitbe? whatcanitbe?
from atop the mausoleum shelf.

Global Positioning

for J.

Give the deliveryman his dream:
good directions, patched potholes,
twenty blocks of traffic lights turning green;
let his shoulders unhunch after the asshole cuts him off;
monitor the truck behind picking up speed.
Let him stay keen at school crosswalks,
and ease left when the cyclist swerves.

He's a decent man, brakes long
before a texting teen jaywalks in his path
smiles politely at the corner at the pretty girl's
sidelong glance to his nod to proceed.

The pedestrian plod goes on, red light
or green; a man has no boss in a car;
he can notice a moonrise: round and full
in the east, that mist at sunset
makes asphalt gleam, how headlights
strung along the elevated highway split the sky:
purple clouds becoming mountain range
black ones carving city scape
into a perfect valley, newly-made.

5th Grade Homework: Make a Serf Costume

for T.

Jails, not manor houses, were built for lads like you;
poor and pre-pubescent, you tell me, the after-school tutor lady,
how you won't wear pantyhose to tomorrow's history class;
nor will you be shepherd, guilds' man, farmer;
instead you mime tucking a sword into your waistband.
Beware, school district sheriffs are harsh!
Resist, mouth off or act out, your little mom will weep!
They'll banish you to the part of the ward
for the ne'er-do-well boys, where dreams die!

I agree; it's insulting, the play-acting, the peasant-boy bow,
to the lord of the manor; learning how the workingman's profit
ends up at the counting house.

What, teacher has chosen a girl to be king?
(Re crowns: The Department of Education
serves existing princes and princesses best,
for them drawbridges are lowered, gleaming carriages welcomed;
how else justify the number of high school slots
is not equal to the number of junior high school students?)

"Tell," asked last month's reading test, "a secret someone's told you."
Give details in your essay; make your argument convincing,
your final mark depends on it!
The Common Core Literary Standard asks you to reveal:
your family's green card status,
whatever drunken uncles might be in the mix, incest?
Must be four paragraphs!

You've never met your brown-skinned Turkish father?
but you say you'd rather be all Puerto Rican.
Like the city he's from, this neighborhood spans two continents:
in one, sunlight sparkles on the roofs of golden palaces,
in the other, boys, in hand-me-down tunics, pine for McDonald's.

Hareem Girls in Moonlight

for S.

It is expected tonight the scuff
of the master's jeweled slipper stops
outside the new girl's door.
She's from the south we hear;
rare to find such beauty there,
the land's so parched skin shrivels
early on the bone; she must be young.

The right guard has been bribed,
we'll wait for the sun to slip down,
before we slip away ourselves,
I knew, when they brought her here, we'd go!

At the baths today how the old ones fussed:
oh, such eyes! That mane of hair!
A form exactly like their own once was!
We've heard it all before—hundreds of girls,
fresh from some dusty hill have shivered
just as shyly beneath the sponge.
Here, where we plot, slave against slave,
for the fate of sons, where servants
offer sweetmeats to the toothless crones,
where eunuchs lock the doors,
or open them, as master's tread prefers.

It will be glorious tonight!
Last time there we cast our robes on shore,
rushed in, how clear the water was!
It seemed we swam the moon's full path,
so fresh the air, not like this
humid, perfumed cave of female musk.

She couldn't know a thing but sheep herd
and work–she'll quickly learn; girlish trembling's
soon replaced by the favorite's strut.
I was passed, crone-to-crone,
giddy from the bathhouse steam,

my stomach still in knots from the awful clank
of coins in father's hand, the daggers
all the soldiers wore; their wolfen eyes.

In the harbor waves lap golden
against the merchant hulls.
No other city shines,
or straddles Europe's spine like this!

He wrapped fat legs around my waist,
called me his—what could I know of kings?
I was a child! A game to him, my torture-won
response, his need to make me feel something
deep inside, that was his conquest, his prize.

Our life's the stuff of ballads, I know:
we lounge, oiled and glittering on silken
pillows, silken rugs, so the shepherd's pipe trills.
Villages and huts have their own system of value;
and our jewels, meted out to guards,
over a lifetime, are unrenewable.

The moon rises above the garden wall,
the lock springs open, the giant gives the sign!
come, sisters, exit like the ghosts we are,
soon the shore will bloom with cast-off veils.
What joy to steal away!

She has yet to know how poison makes
a rival writhe, that the youngest will supplant her,
how tenuously we stand with our sons
in the line of heirs; but tonight, without jailors,
let's wend our way to the waterside,
paddle steadfastly out, past
where the fishing boats are buffeted by the tide;
dive down beneath a golden sea turned black,
rise up, laughing sisters, by each other's side,
breasts turned up like mirrors to the moon,
those famous domes faint shadows against the sky.

Words for Everything

*Look at all this beauty, truth and emotion created
from nothing but words. Just words. How can you
possibly spend your life not trying to do the same?'*

Lampedusa

We like attention, my mother and I,
a whistle, flattery, to see attraction
in a stranger's eye; old geishas, we laugh
with painted lips, gaze through
dark-rimmed eyes and like this
disorder of petals in the July Botanic Garden,
we're fading, too.

Her mania, born as happy chatter first,
becomes a storm of words; sentences
unfurl and at the end of each she says
my name, my name, my name! (What
syllables call fallen daughters back
from detachment this deep?)
When the fanciful label of every rose
is spoken, ascends, buzzes past my ear,
and scatters through the lattice fence,
I know she's off her meds again.

In the short silence between each pause
for breath I must agree: Yes, Mother!
Yes! The ibis (perched serenely
by the lake) does seem embalmed,
that bit of sludge beneath the span
makes the little bridge a mess! I did have
such a cheery youth, you bet!

Remember me as good she longs to say,
as beautiful and just, but tilts her head away
to compliment a peony instead, whose blossoms
hushed at least a month, seems mute.

The sun goes in; I shrink my stride to match
her tiny steps; we're on the path where the old cherry trees
were wrenched; I knew them well, but missed the week

these young ones first turned pink; could there be rain?
or will these clouds blow East?

She says my father's ghost invited her to heaven last night;
but she refused! In the dream he was handsome
and young, she chirps, eyes radiant;
in her face the dream of us
in a garden of love, still full.

Running in the Winter Park

Running in the winter park
you learn to have a relationship
with cold, stark tree limbs, white sky,
windy hills; forget your watch, forgo
measurement of each footfall's length;
breath turns to thought in your chest:

the frozen lake has its summer paddlers back,
the narrow path where a woman stopped to pluck
a leaf from her daughter's hair, is strewn again
with gold; you mark the place last spring's
runaway horse ended his riderless surge;

much further back—a family picnic near
the little waterfall, designed to flow
from pipe to stream, then over
our happy heads; those months last year
when the drone of every plane filled us
with such dread—but here,
the Indian women, saris rivaling sunset,
stood in satin shoes
by the water's edge and there, steps
from the Rose of Sharon, the children's park
where my ailing son learned to walk again.

A hawk circles above the open space
where farmers put their market stalls:

so full the overlap of colors, sounds and scents!
such flowers, jams, cheeses, apples, wool,
I pile my baskets then! It's all here,
in the silence I ruin with every pounding foot
and gasping breath, sometimes enough
to obscure the road I bring here in my head.

Lunes

Artists @ lunch
Smile despite many missing teeth
Their pockets empty

Childhood + Mind = Cloud

One appears in every student poem:
not as ominous; last year's hurricanes
are forgotten; in their drawings
a white puff floats,
a curve of sun smiles over rooftops,
dancing animals galumph across green grass;
a park swing swoops high,
a stick figure mother
extends her tiny star hand.

VIA Folios

A refereed book series dedicated to the culture of Italians and Italian Americans.

FRED GARDAPHÉ. *Read 'em and Reap.* Vol. 123. Criticism. $22
JOSEPH A. AMATO. *Diagnostics.* Vol 122. Literature. $12.
DENNIS BARONE. *Second Thoughts.* Vol 121. Poetry. $10
OLIVIA K. CERRONE. *The Hunger Saint.* Vol 120. Novella. $12
GARIBLADI M. LAPOLLA. *Miss Rollins in Love.* Vol 119. Novel. $24
JOSEPH TUSIANI. *A Clarion Call.* Vol 118. Poetry. $16
JOSEPH A. AMATO. *My Three Sicilies.* Vol 117. Poetry & Prose. $17
MARGHERITA COSTA. *Voice of a Virtuosa and Coutesan.* Vol 116. Poetry. $24
NICOLE SANTALUCIA. *Because I Did Not Die.* Vol 115. Poetry. $12
MARK CIABATTARI. *Preludes to History.* Vol 114. Poetry. $12
HELEN BAROLINI. *Visits.* Vol 113. Novel. $22
ERNESTO LIVORNI. *The Fathers' America.* Vol 112. Poetry. $14
MARIO B. MIGNONE. *The Story of My People.* Vol 111. Non-fiction. $17
GEORGE GUIDA. *The Sleeping Gulf.* Vol 110. Poetry. $14
JOEY NICOLETTI. *Reverse Graffiti.* Vol 109. Poetry. $14
GIOSE RIMANELLI. *Il mestiere del furbo.* Vol 108. Criticism. $20
LEWIS TURCO. *The Hero Enkido.* Vol 107. Poetry. $14
AL TACCONELLI. *Perhaps Fly.* Vol 106. Poetry. $14
RACHEL GUIDO DEVRIES. *A Woman Unknown in Her Bones.* Vol 105. Poetry. $11
BERNARD BRUNO. *A Tear and a Tear in My Heart.* Vol 104. Non-fiction. $20
FELIX STEFANILE. *Songs of the Sparrow.* Vol 103. Poetry. $30
FRANK POLIZZI. *A New Life with Bianca.* Vol 102. Poetry. $10
GIL FAGIANI. *Stone Walls.* Vol 101. Poetry. $14
LOUISE DESALVO. *Casting Off.* Vol 100. Fiction. $22
MARY JO BONA. *I Stop Waiting for You.* Vol 99. Poetry. $12
RACHEL GUIDO DEVRIES. *Stati zitt, Josie.* Vol 98. Children's Literature. $8
GRACE CAVALIERI. *The Mandate of Heaven.* Vol 97. Poetry. $14
MARISA FRASCA. *Via incanto.* Vol 96. Poetry. $12
DOUGLAS GLADSTONE. *Carving a Niche for Himself.* Vol 95. History. $12
MARIA TERRONE. *Eye to Eye.* Vol 94. Poetry. $14
CONSTANCE SANCETTA. *Here in Cerchio.* Vol 93. Local History. $15
MARIA MAZZIOTTI GILLAN. *Ancestors' Song.* Vol 92. Poetry. $14
MICHAEL PARENTI. *Waiting for Yesterday: Pages from a Street Kid's Life.* Vol 90. Memoir. $15
ANNIE LANZILLOTTO. *Schistsong.* Vol 89. Poetry. $15
EMANUEL DI PASQUALE. *Love Lines.* Vol 88. Poetry. $10
CAROSONE & LOGIUDICE. *Our Naked Lives.* Vol 87. Essays. $15

JAMES PERICONI. *Strangers in a Strange Land: A Survey of Italian-Language American Books.*Vol 86. Book History. $24

DANIELA GIOSEFFI. *Escaping La Vita Della Cucina*. Vol 85. Essays. $22

MARIA FAMÀ. *Mystics in the Family*. Vol 84. Poetry. $10

ROSSANA DEL ZIO. *From Bread and Tomatoes to Zuppa di Pesce "Ciambotto"*.Vol. 83. $15

LORENZO DELBOCA. *Polentoni*. Vol 82. Italian Studies. $15

SAMUEL GHELLI. *A Reference Grammar*. Vol 81. Italian Language. $36

ROSS TALARICO. *Sled Run*. Vol 80. Fiction. $15

FRED MISURELLA. *Only Sons*. Vol 79. Fiction. $14

FRANK LENTRICCHIA. *The Portable Lentricchia*. Vol 78. Fiction. $16

RICHARD VETERE. *The Other Colors in a Snow Storm*. Vol 77. Poetry. $10

GARIBALDI LAPOLLA. *Fire in the Flesh*. Vol 76 Fiction & Criticism. $25

GEORGE GUIDA. *The Pope Stories*. Vol 75 Prose. $15

ROBERT VISCUSI. *Ellis Island*. Vol 74. Poetry. $28

ELENA GIANINI BELOTTI. *The Bitter Taste of Strangers Bread*. Vol 73. Fiction. $24

PINO APRILE. *Terroni*. Vol 72. Italian Studies. $20

EMANUEL DI PASQUALE. *Harvest*. Vol 71. Poetry. $10

ROBERT ZWEIG. *Return to Naples*. Vol 70. Memoir. $16

AIROS & CAPPELLI. *Guido*. Vol 69. Italian/American Studies. $12

FRED GARDAPHÉ. *Moustache Pete is Dead! Long Live Moustache Pete!.* Vol 67. Literature/Oral History. $12

PAOLO RUFFILLI. *Dark Room/Camera oscura*. Vol 66. Poetry. $11

HELEN BAROLINI. *Crossing the Alps*. Vol 65. Fiction. $14

COSMO FERRARA. *Profiles of Italian Americans*. Vol 64. Italian Americana. $16

GIL FAGIANI. *Chianti in Connecticut*. Vol 63. Poetry. $10

BASSETTI & D'ACQUINO. *Italic Lessons*. Vol 62. Italian/American Studies. $10

CAVALIERI & PASCARELLI, Eds. *The Poet's Cookbook*. Vol 61. Poetry/Recipes. $12

EMANUEL DI PASQUALE. *Siciliana*. Vol 60. Poetry. $8

NATALIA COSTA, Ed. *Bufalini*. Vol 59. Poetry. $18.

RICHARD VETERE. *Baroque*. Vol 58. Fiction. $18.

LEWIS TURCO. *La Famiglia/The Family*. Vol 57. Memoir. $15

NICK JAMES MILETI. *The Unscrupulous*. Vol 56. Humanities. $20

BASSETTI. ACCOLLA. D'AQUINO. *Italici: An Encounter with Piero Bassetti*. Vol 55. Italian Studies. $8

GIOSE RIMANELLI. *The Three-legged One*. Vol 54. Fiction. $15

CHARLES KLOPP. *Bele Antiche Stòrie*. Vol 53. Criticism. $25

JOSEPH RICAPITO. *Second Wave*. Vol 52. Poetry. $12

GARY MORMINO. *Italians in Florida*. Vol 51. History. $15

GIANFRANCO ANGELUCCI. *Federico F*. Vol 50. Fiction. $15

ANTHONY VALERIO. *The Little Sailor*. Vol 49. Memoir. $9

ROSS TALARICO. *The Reptilian Interludes*. Vol 48. Poetry. $15

RACHEL GUIDO DE VRIES. *Teeny Tiny Tino's Fishing Story*. Vol 47. Children's Literature. $6

EMANUEL DI PASQUALE. *Writing Anew*. Vol 46. Poetry. $15

MARIA FAMÀ. *Looking For Cover*. Vol 45. Poetry. $12

ANTHONY VALERIO. *Toni Cade Bambara's One Sicilian Night*. Vol 44. Poetry. $10

EMANUEL CARNEVALI. *Furnished Rooms*. Vol 43. Poetry. $14

BRENT ADKINS. et al., Ed. *Shifting Borders. Negotiating Places*. Vol 42. Conference. $18

GEORGE GUIDA. *Low Italian*. Vol 41. Poetry. $11

GARDAPHÈ, GIORDANO, TAMBURRI. *Introducing Italian Americana*. Vol 40. Italian/American Studies. $10

DANIELA GIOSEFFI. *Blood Autumn/Autunno di sangue*. Vol 39. Poetry. $15/$25

FRED MISURELLA. *Lies to Live By*. Vol 38. Stories. $15

STEVEN BELLUSCIO. *Constructing a Bibliography*. Vol 37. Italian Americana. $15

ANTHONY JULIAN TAMBURRI, Ed. *Italian Cultural Studies 2002*. Vol 36. Essays. $18

BEA TUSIANI. *con amore*. Vol 35. Memoir. $19

FLAVIA BRIZIO-SKOV, Ed. *Reconstructing Societies in the Aftermath of War*. Vol 34. History. $30

TAMBURRI. et al., Eds. *Italian Cultural Studies 2001*. Vol 33. Essays. $18

ELIZABETH G. MESSINA, Ed. *In Our Own Voices*. Vol 32. Italian/American Studies. $25

STANISLAO G. PUGLIESE. *Desperate Inscriptions*. Vol 31. History. $12

HOSTERT & TAMBURRI, Eds. *Screening Ethnicity*. Vol 30. Italian/American Culture. $25

G. PARATI & B. LAWTON, Eds. *Italian Cultural Studies*. Vol 29. Essays. $18

HELEN BAROLINI. *More Italian Hours*. Vol 28. Fiction. $16

FRANCO NASI, Ed. *Intorno alla Via Emilia*. Vol 27. Culture. $16

ARTHUR L. CLEMENTS. *The Book of Madness & Love*. Vol 26. Poetry. $10

JOHN CASEY, et al. *Imagining Humanity*. Vol 25. Interdisciplinary Studies. $18

ROBERT LIMA. *Sardinia/Sardegna*. Vol 24. Poetry. $10

DANIELA GIOSEFFI. *Going On*. Vol 23. Poetry. $10

ROSS TALARICO. *The Journey Home*. Vol 22. Poetry. $12

EMANUEL DI PASQUALE. *The Silver Lake Love Poems*. Vol 21. Poetry. $7

JOSEPH TUSIANI. *Ethnicity*. Vol 20. Poetry. $12

JENNIFER LAGIER. *Second Class Citizen*. Vol 19. Poetry. $8

FELIX STEFANILE. *The Country of Absence*. Vol 18. Poetry. $9

PHILIP CANNISTRARO. *Blackshirts*. Vol 17. History. $12

LUIGI RUSTICHELLI, Ed. *Seminario sul racconto*. Vol 16. Narrative. $10

LEWIS TURCO. *Shaking the Family Tree*. Vol 15. Memoirs. $9

LUIGI RUSTICHELLI, Ed. *Seminario sulla drammaturgia*. Vol 14. Theater/ Essays. $10

FRED GARDAPHÈ. *Moustache Pete is Dead! Long Live Moustache Pete!*. Vol 13. Oral Literature. $10

JONE GAILLARD CORSI. *Il libretto d'autore. 1860–1930*. Vol 12. Criticism. $17

HELEN BAROLINI. *Chiaroscuro: Essays of Identity*. Vol 11. Essays. $15

PICARAZZI & FEINSTEIN, Eds. *An African Harlequin in Milan*. Vol 10. Theater/Essays. $15

JOSEPH RICAPITO. *Florentine Streets & Other Poems*. Vol 9. Poetry. $9

FRED MISURELLA. *Short Time*. Vol 8. Novella. $7

NED CONDINI. *Quartettsatz*. Vol 7. Poetry. $7

ANTHONY JULIAN TAMBURRI, Ed. *Fuori: Essays by Italian/American Lesbiansand Gays*. Vol 6. Essays. $10

ANTONIO GRAMSCI. P. Verdicchio. Trans. & Intro. *The Southern Question*. Vol 5.Social Criticism. $5

DANIELA GIOSEFFI. *Word Wounds & Water Flowers*. Vol 4. Poetry. $8

WILEY FEINSTEIN. *Humility's Deceit: Calvino Reading Ariosto Reading Calvino*. Vol 3. Criticism. $10

PAOLO A. GIORDANO, Ed. *Joseph Tusiani: Poet. Translator. Humanist*. Vol 2. Criticism. $25

ROBERT VISCUSI. *Oration Upon the Most Recent Death of Christopher Columbus*. Vol 1. Poetry.

www.ingramcontent.com/pod-product-compliance
Lightning Source LLC
Chambersburg PA
CBHW032057040426
42449CB00007B/1110

* 9 7 8 1 5 9 9 5 4 1 0 8 2 *